Rookie Read-About® Science

Flies Are Fascinating

By Valerie Wilkinson

Consultants:
Robert L. Hillerich, Professor Emeritus,
Bowling Green State University, Bowling Green, Ohio
Consultant, Pinellas County Schools, Florida

Lynne Kepler, Educational Consultant

Fay Robinson, Child Development Specialist

SCHOLASTIC INC.
New York Toronto London Auckland Sydney
Mexico City New Delhi Hong Kong Buenos Aires

ISBN 0-516-24113-3

Copyright © 1994 by Children's Press®, Inc.
All rights reserved.
Published by Scholastic Inc., 555 Broadway, New York, NY 10012.
SCHOLASTIC and associated logos are trademarks and/or registered trademarks of Scholastic Inc.

24 23 22 21 20 19 18 17 16   14 15 16 17 18 19/0

Printed in the United States of America   08

Design by Lindaanne Donohoe

Most adult insects fly.

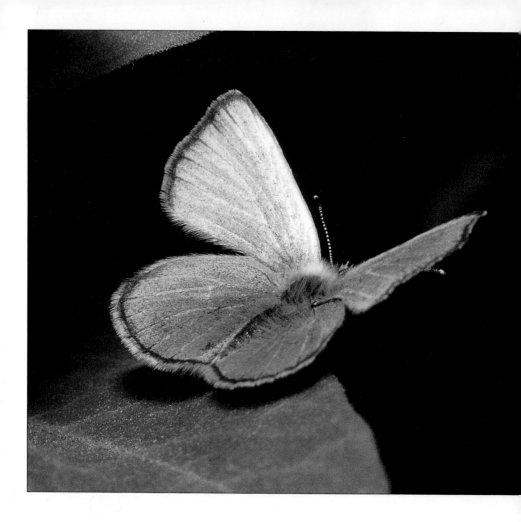

Butterflies have four
beautifully colored wings.

Dragonflies have four delicate, gauzy wings.

But true flies have only
two wings.

Di is a Greek word meaning "two."
Ptera is a Greek word meaning "wings."

Flies belong to the order Diptera.

There are more than 85,000 different kinds of true flies.

Houseflies, deerflies, mosquitoes, horseflies, blackflies, and gnats

are true flies.

A fly folds its wings

on top of its body.

Look closely at this fly's head.

It has huge eyes.

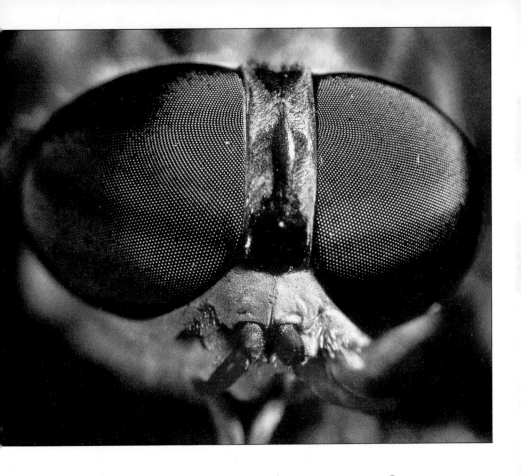

They are made up of
many tiny lenses and are
called compound eyes.

Some flies, like this
housefly, are dark colored.

Some are brightly colored
with a metallic shine.

We call these flies
bluebottles or greenbottles.

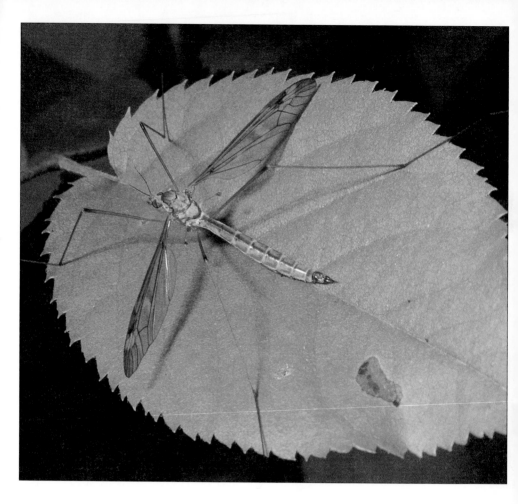

Some flies are large like
this crane fly.

Some flies are tiny like
this fruit fly at right.

Some harmless flies
imitate other insects.

The hover or syrphid fly
has yellow and black
stripes so we will think
it carries a sting . . .
like a bee or a wasp.

Flies do not sting, but
many bite.

Female blackflies, deerflies, mosquitoes, and horseflies bite animals to suck the

blood that they need for their eggs.

They bite people too.

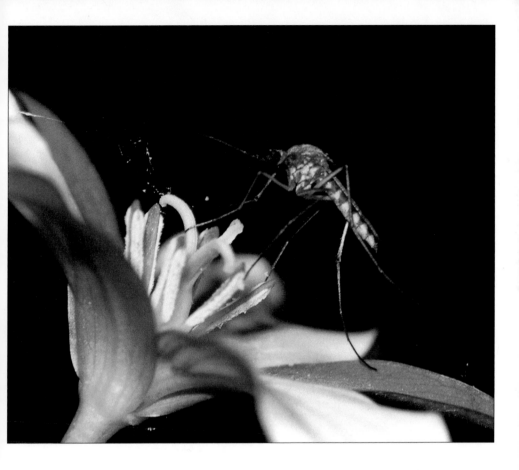

Male flies do not bother
people. They feed only
on plants.

Flies do not make nests
like wasps or bees.

They lay their eggs
on food, on water,
on the ground, or
on other animals.

The eggs hatch into larvae.
Fly larvae are often white.

We call them maggots.

Mosquitoes are most common where there is water.

Mosquito larvae hang upside down just beneath the water's surface.

They breathe air through a tiny tube.

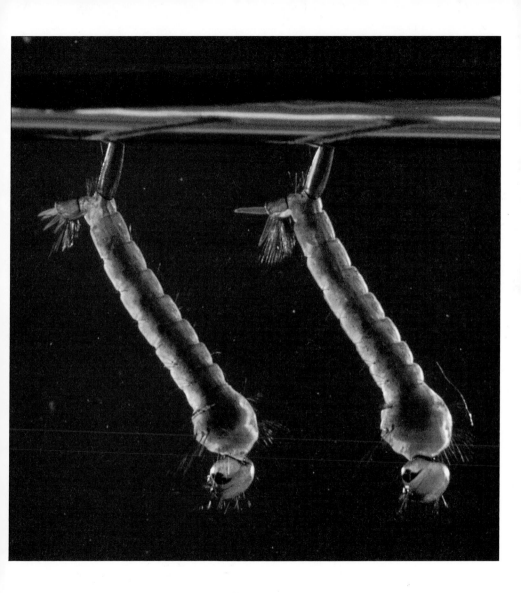

Fish and other underwater animals eat millions of these mosquito larvae.

That's good.

There are fewer mosquitoes left to bother us.

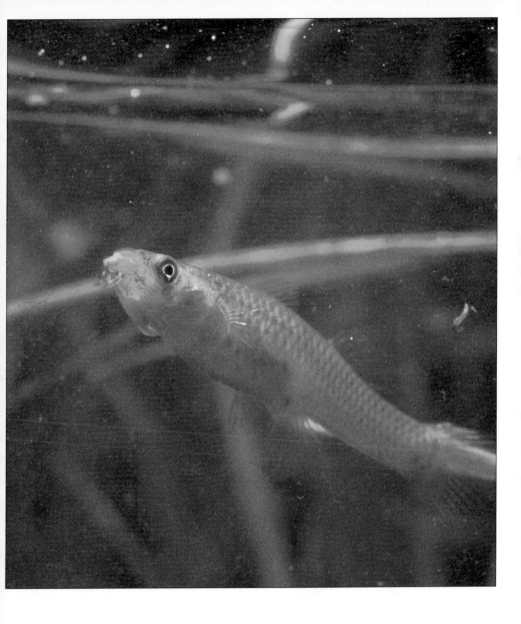

Adult flies are often eaten by spiders, other insects, birds, and animals.

Who
would have
imagined
that flies
are such
tasty food
for so
many
creatures?

Words You Know
Diptera

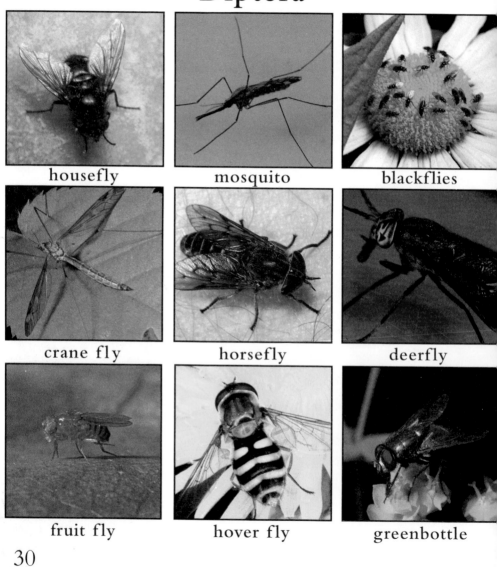

housefly

mosquito

blackflies

crane fly

horsefly

deerfly

fruit fly

hover fly

greenbottle

folded wings

wings in flight

fly head

compound eyes

fly eggs

maggots

mosquito larvae

31

Index

About the Author

Valerie Wilkinson worked for ten years as an industrial chemist before leaving England to travel in Europe and Africa photographing and writing on environmental topics. She is the founder and manager of VALAN PHOTOS, a stock photo agency in Ontario, Canada that specializes in wildlife and environmental photography.

Photo Credits

Animals Animals – ©R.H. Armstrong, 3; ©G.I. Bernard, 15, 30 (bottom left); ©C.W. Perkins, 25, 30 (center right), 31 (bottom right); ©E.R. Degginger, 30 (top center); ©Stephen Dalton, 31 (top right)

Macro/Nature Photography – ©Robert F. Sisson, 27

Tom Stack & Associates – ©Rod Planck, Cover; ©David M. Dennis, 6, 30 (top left); ©Richard P. Smith, 8; ©Kerry T. Givens, 11, 31 (center right)

Valan – ©G.L. Christie, 4; ©V.&A. Wilkinson, 5, 9, 13, 30 (bottom right), 31 (top left); ©J.R. Page, 10, 18, 31 (center left); ©J.A. Wilkinson, 12, 30 (center center), ©John Fowler, 14, 21, 30 (top right, center left); ©Michel Bourque, 17, 30 (bottom center); ©Fred Bruemmer, 19; ©John Eastcott/Yva Momatiuk, 20; ©Jim Merli, 28; ©Wayne Lankinen, 29

Visuals Unlimited – ©R.F. Ashley, 22, 31 (bottom left); ©Bill Beatty, 23, 31 (bottom center)

COVER: Flesh fly